THE DAILY FEELINGS JOURNAL FOR KIDS

FOR KIDS

A Year of Prompts to Help Kids Recognize Emotions and Express Feelings

NATHAN GREENE, PsyD

ROCKRIDGE
PRESS

Interior and Cover Designer: Alan Carr
Art Producer: Alyssa Williams
Editor: Laura Bryn Sisson
Production Editor: Jael Fogle
Production Manager: Jose Olivera

All illustrations used under license from istock.com

Paperback ISBN: 978-1-63878-070-0
R0

This Journal Belongs to

_____

INTRODUCTION

Welcome to your feelings journal! You may have gotten this book because your feelings are big or overwhelming. Or maybe you are just curious about them.

Sometimes when feelings are hard for us, we may think, "My feelings are the enemy!"

But here's a little secret about feelings: If we become friends with our feelings, they will no longer be our enemies. Every feeling—whether it's joy, frustration, sadness, or any other—carries important information. When we learn to recognize our feelings, understand them, and express them in a healthy way, they can become helpful tools for learning about ourselves and the world around us. They can become a kind of superpower.

Feelings . . . a superpower? Yes! All feelings, positive or negative, have important messages for us. When we listen to them, feelings can guide us to what we need and how to get it.

The Daily Feelings Journal for Kids will help you befriend your feelings so you can harness their power. You will find spaces to write about your feelings every day and a weekly prompt to help you dive deeper into a specific feeling or theme. You will also find suggestions for real-life activities and a mood log for every day of the month. You can start the journal on whatever day it is today. Just circle the day of the week and write in the date.

I'm excited for you to begin your feelings journey! How do you feel? Turn the page to the first prompt to get to the bottom of it.

Write about a time recently when you felt happy. What did you feel in your body?

_____

_____

_____

_____

_____

_____

_____

_____

_____

Feelings Challenge!

Find your joy! Play a song that makes you happy and dance to it.

Smile Tracker!

This week, I smiled when _____

_____

_____

Explore your emotions! Write about the feelings that you experience each day, and why you felt them.

| M T W T F S S | ___/___/___ |

| M T W T F S S | ___/___/___ |

| M T W T F S S | ___/___/___ |

| M T W T F S S | ___/___/___ |

| M T W T F S S | ___/___/___ |

| M T W T F S S | ___/___/___ |

| M T W T F S S | ___/___/___ |

If your anger were a character, who would it be and why?

_____

_____

_____

_____

_____

_____

_____

Feelings Challenge!

The next time you get angry, follow these three steps:

1. Take a deep breath to slow down your heart rate.

2. Say why you are feeling angry out loud in a calm voice.

3. Think of the character you came up with to represent your anger and picture them doing something funny to help lessen the feeling.

Smile Tracker!

This week, I smiled when _____

_____

_____

Explore your emotions! Write about the feelings that you experience each day, and why you felt them.

M T W T F S S   ___ / ___ / ___

M T W T F S S   ___ / ___ / ___

M T W T F S S   ___ / ___ / ___

M T W T F S S   ___ / ___ / ___

M T W T F S S   ___ / ___ / ___

M T W T F S S   ___ / ___ / ___

M T W T F S S   ___ / ___ / ___

When was the last time you felt sad? What helped you feel better?

_____

_____

_____

_____

_____

_____

_____

_____

Feelings Challenge!

Play feelings charades with your family. Act out different feelings and guess what they are.

Smile Tracker!

This week, I smiled when _____

_____

_____

Explore your emotions! Write about the feelings that you experience each day, and why you felt them.

M T W T F S S   ___ / ___ / ___

M T W T F S S   ___ / ___ / ___

M T W T F S S   ___ / ___ / ___

M T W T F S S   ___ / ___ / ___

M T W T F S S   ___ / ___ / ___

M T W T F S S   ___ / ___ / ___

M T W T F S S   ___ / ___ / ___

Write about a time when you felt embarrassed. What did you want to do?

_____

_____

_____

_____

_____

_____

_____

_____

_____

Feelings Challenge!

Ask an adult to tell you about a time when they felt embarrassed at your age.

Smile Tracker!

This week, I smiled when _____

_____

_____

Explore your emotions! Write about the feelings that you experience each day, and why you felt them.

M T W T F S S   ___/___/___

M T W T F S S   ___/___/___

M T W T F S S   ___/___/___

Think of a feeling you had this month. Imagine if that feeling were a character. Draw a picture of that feelings character and include a bubble showing what they might think or say.

Mood Log for the Month of
_____!

Each box below represents a day this month. Every day draw how you feel.

HAPPY	SAD	SILLY	ANGRY	DISAPPOINTED	FRUSTRATED
GRATEFUL	ANXIOUS	SURPRISED	EXCITED	SCARED	PROUD

1	2	3	4	5	6	7
8	9	10	11	12	13	14
15	16	17	18	19	20	21
22	23	24	25	26	27	28
29	30	31				

What was the feeling you had the most this month? _____

_____

Explore your emotions! Write about the feelings that you experience each day, and why you felt them.

M T W T F S S   ___ / ___ / ___

M T W T F S S   ___ / ___ / ___

M T W T F S S   ___ / ___ / ___

M T W T F S S   ___ / ___ / ___

M T W T F S S   ___ / ___ / ___

M T W T F S S   ___ / ___ / ___

M T W T F S S   ___ / ___ / ___

If your joy were a character, who would it be and why?

_____

_____

_____

_____

_____

_____

_____

_____

_____

_____

Feelings Challenge!

Make up a song about something that brings you joy, and sing it to someone you know.

Smile Tracker!

This week, I smiled when _____

_____

_____

Explore your emotions! Write about the feelings that you experience each day, and why you felt them.

M T W T F S S   ___ / ___ / ___

M T W T F S S   ___ / ___ / ___

M T W T F S S   ___ / ___ / ___

M T W T F S S   ___ / ___ / ___

M T W T F S S   ___ / ___ / ___

M T W T F S S   ___ / ___ / ___

M T W T F S S   ___ / ___ / ___

Write about a time when you felt dread about going to school and why.

_____

_____

_____

_____

_____

_____

_____

_____

_____

Feelings Challenge!

Fill a box or a bag with a few items that will help you feel better at school.

Smile Tracker!

This week, I smiled when _____

_____

_____

Explore your emotions! Write about the feelings that you experience each day, and why you felt them.

M T W T F S S   ___/___/___

M T W T F S S   ___/___/___

M T W T F S S   ___/___/___

M T W T F S S   ___/___/___

M T W T F S S   ___/___/___

M T W T F S S   ___/___/___

M T W T F S S   ___/___/___

When was the last time you felt disappointed? What helped you feel better?

_____

_____

_____

_____

_____

_____

_____

_____

Feelings Challenge!

Pretend another kid experienced the same disappointment you did. Practice saying things in front of a mirror that would help them feel better.

Smile Tracker!

This week, I smiled when _____

_____

_____

Explore your emotions! Write about the feelings that you experience each day, and why you felt them.

M T W T F S S   ___/___/___

M T W T F S S   ___/___/___

M T W T F S S   ___/___/___

M T W T F S S   ___/___/___

M T W T F S S   ___/___/___

M T W T F S S   ___/___/___

M T W T F S S   ___/___/___

Write about what pride feels like in your face, hands, and chest.

_____

_____

_____

_____

_____

_____

_____

_____

Feelings Challenge!

Think of three things that you love about yourself. Find a mirror, put your hand on your heart, and say these things to yourself in front of the mirror. Notice how you feel.

Smile Tracker!

This week, I smiled when _____

_____

_____

Explore your emotions! Write about the feelings that you experience each day, and why you felt them.

M T W T F S S   ___ /___ /___

M T W T F S S   ___ /___ /___

M T W T F S S   ___ /___ /___

Think of a feeling you had this month. Imagine if that feeling were a character. Draw a picture of that feelings character and include a bubble showing what they might think or say.

Mood Log for the Month of
_____!

Each box below represents a day this month. Every day draw how you feel.

HAPPY	SAD	SILLY	ANGRY	DISAPPOINTED	FRUSTRATED
GRATEFUL	ANXIOUS	SURPRISED	EXCITED	SCARED	PROUD

1	2	3	4	5	6	7
8	9	10	11	12	13	14
15	16	17	18	19	20	21
22	23	24	25	26	27	28
29	30	31				

What was the feeling you had the most this month? _____

_____

Explore your emotions! Write about the feelings that you experience each day, and why you felt them.

MTWTFSS   ___/___/___

MTWTFSS   ___/___/___

MTWTFSS   ___/___/___

MTWTFSS   ___/___/___

MTWTFSS   ___/___/___

MTWTFSS   ___/___/___

MTWTFSS   ___/___/___

Write about a recent time you were frustrated. What did it make you want to do?

_____

_____

_____

_____

_____

_____

_____

_____

Feelings Challenge!

Next time you're upset, ask yourself if you're HALTED? (Hungry? Angry? Lonely? Tired? Embarrassed? Disappointed?) This will help you know what you need.

Smile Tracker!

This week, I smiled when _____

_____

_____

Explore your emotions! Write about the feelings that you experience each day, and why you felt them.

M T W T F S S   ___/___/___

M T W T F S S   ___/___/___

M T W T F S S   ___/___/___

M T W T F S S   ___/___/___

M T W T F S S   ___/___/___

M T W T F S S   ___/___/___

M T W T F S S   ___/___/___

Write a short poem comparing your anger with objects in the real world. For example: "My anger is like a volcano spewing molten lava."

_____

_____

_____

_____

_____

_____

_____

_____

Feelings Challenge!

Interview one friend and one family member about what helps them calm down when they're angry.

Smile Tracker!

This week, I smiled when _____

_____

_____

Explore your emotions! Write about the feelings that you experience each day, and why you felt them.

M T W T F S S   ___ / ___ / ___

M T W T F S S   ___ / ___ / ___

M T W T F S S   ___ / ___ / ___

M T W T F S S   ___ / ___ / ___

M T W T F S S   ___ / ___ / ___

M T W T F S S   ___ / ___ / ___

M T W T F S S   ___ / ___ / ___

Write about a time when you felt proud of yourself. How did your body feel?

_____

_____

_____

_____

_____

_____

_____

_____

_____

Feelings Challenge!

Tell a friend about an accomplishment, big or small, that you are proud of.

Smile Tracker!

This week, I smiled when _____

_____

_____

Explore your emotions! Write about the feelings that you experience each day, and why you felt them.

M T W T F S S   ___/___/___

M T W T F S S   ___/___/___

M T W T F S S   ___/___/___

M T W T F S S   ___/___/___

M T W T F S S   ___/___/___

M T W T F S S   ___/___/___

M T W T F S S   ___/___/___

Write a short poem about a time when you felt really, extremely embarrassed.

_____

_____

_____

_____

_____

_____

_____

_____

Feelings Challenge!

Next time you feel embarrassed, take a deep breath. Then, remind yourself you are probably not the only person this has ever happened to.

Smile Tracker!

This week, I smiled when _____

_____

_____

Explore your emotions! Write about the feelings that you experience each day, and why you felt them.

| M T W T F S S | ___/___/___ |

| M T W T F S S | ___/___/___ |

| M T W T F S S | ___/___/___ |

Think of a feeling you had this month. Imagine if that feeling were a character. Draw a picture of that feelings character and include a bubble showing what they might think or say.

Mood Log for the Month of

_____!

Each box below represents a day this month. Every day draw how you feel.

HAPPY	SAD	SILLY	ANGRY	DISAPPOINTED	FRUSTRATED
GRATEFUL	ANXIOUS	SURPRISED	EXCITED	SCARED	PROUD

1	2	3	4	5	6	7
8	9	10	11	12	13	14
15	16	17	18	19	20	21
22	23	24	25	26	27	28
29	30	31				

What was the feeling you had the most this month? _____

_____

Explore your emotions! Write about the feelings that you experience each day, and why you felt them.

M T W T F S S ___/___/___

M T W T F S S ___/___/___

M T W T F S S ___/___/___

M T W T F S S ___/___/___

M T W T F S S ___/___/___

M T W T F S S ___/___/___

M T W T F S S ___/___/___

When you are excited, what do you feel in your hands? In your face? How about in your stomach?

_____

_____

_____

_____

_____

_____

_____

_____

Feelings Challenge!

Play a song that pumps you up with excitement, and move the way the song makes you feel. Then, play a calming song and see how your body moves differently.

Smile Tracker!

This week, I smiled when _____

_____

_____

Explore your emotions! Write about the feelings that you experience each day, and why you felt them.

M T W T F S S ___/___/___

M T W T F S S ___/___/___

M T W T F S S ___/___/___

M T W T F S S ___/___/___

M T W T F S S ___/___/___

M T W T F S S ___/___/___

M T W T F S S ___/___/___

What are three things that you appreciate about your health?

_____

_____

_____

_____

_____

_____

_____

_____

_____

Feelings Challenge!

Write a letter to your body thanking it for the good things it does for you.

Smile Tracker!

This week, I smiled when _____

_____

_____

Explore your emotions! Write about the feelings that you experience each day, and why you felt them.

M T W T F S S   ___/___/___

M T W T F S S   ___/___/___

M T W T F S S   ___/___/___

M T W T F S S   ___/___/___

M T W T F S S   ___/___/___

M T W T F S S   ___/___/___

M T W T F S S   ___/___/___

When was the last time you felt really scared? What was something that helped you feel better?

_____

_____

_____

_____

_____

_____

_____

_____

_____

Feelings Challenge!

Imagine a scene that helps you feel calm. It can be from real life or you can make one up!

Smile Tracker!

This week, I smiled when _____

_____

_____

Explore your emotions! Write about the feelings that you experience each day, and why you felt them.

M T W T F S S   ___/___/___

M T W T F S S   ___/___/___

M T W T F S S   ___/___/___

M T W T F S S   ___/___/___

M T W T F S S   ___/___/___

M T W T F S S   ___/___/___

M T W T F S S   ___/___/___

Identify three feelings you're feeling right now. What colors would they be and why?

_____

_____

_____

_____

_____

_____

_____

_____

Feelings Challenge!

Next time you have a strong feeling, try to identify its color and texture. Does it seem red, or black, or maybe yellow? Is it thick and sticky like a black goop, or is it maybe as light as air?

Smile Tracker!

This week, I smiled when _____

_____

_____

Explore your emotions! Write about the feelings that you experience each day, and why you felt them.

| M T W T F S S | ___ / ___ / ___ |

| M T W T F S S | ___ / ___ / ___ |

| M T W T F S S | ___ / ___ / ___ |

Think of a feeling you had this month. Imagine if that feeling were a character. Draw a picture of that feelings character and include a bubble showing what they might think or say.

Mood Log for the Month of

_____ !

Each box below represents a day this month. Every day draw how you feel.

HAPPY	SAD	SILLY	ANGRY	DISAPPOINTED	FRUSTRATED

GRATEFUL	ANXIOUS	SURPRISED	EXCITED	SCARED	PROUD

1	2	3	4	5	6	7
8	9	10	11	12	13	14
15	16	17	18	19	20	21
22	23	24	25	26	27	28
29	30	31				

What was the feeling you had the most this month? _____

_____

Explore your emotions! Write about the feelings that you
experience each day, and why you felt them.

M T W T F S S   ___ / ___ / ___

M T W T F S S   ___ / ___ / ___

M T W T F S S   ___ / ___ / ___

M T W T F S S   ___ / ___ / ___

M T W T F S S   ___ / ___ / ___

M T W T F S S   ___ / ___ / ___

M T W T F S S   ___ / ___ / ___

Who do you get the silliest with? What silly things have you done?

_____

_____

_____

_____

_____

_____

_____

_____

_____

Feelings Challenge!

Have a funny-face contest with a friend or sibling. See who laughs first!

Smile Tracker!

This week, I smiled when _____

_____

_____

Explore your emotions! Write about the feelings that you experience each day, and why you felt them.

M T W T F S S   ___ / ___ / ___

M T W T F S S   ___ / ___ / ___

M T W T F S S   ___ / ___ / ___

M T W T F S S   ___ / ___ / ___

M T W T F S S   ___ / ___ / ___

M T W T F S S   ___ / ___ / ___

M T W T F S S   ___ / ___ / ___

Write about a choice that you regret making.

_____

_____

_____

_____

_____

_____

_____

_____

_____

_____

Feelings Challenge!

Touching your heart, say to yourself three times, "Good people sometimes make bad choices."

Smile Tracker!

This week, I smiled when _____

_____

_____

Explore your emotions! Write about the feelings that you experience each day, and why you felt them.

M T W T F S S _____/_____/_____

M T W T F S S _____/_____/_____

M T W T F S S _____/_____/_____

M T W T F S S _____/_____/_____

M T W T F S S _____/_____/_____

M T W T F S S _____/_____/_____

M T W T F S S _____/_____/_____

How is "surprised" a different feeling from "shocked"?

_____

_____

_____

_____

_____

_____

_____

_____

_____

_____

Feelings Challenge!

Plan a small surprise for someone you love and make
it happen!

Smile Tracker!

This week, I smiled when _____

_____

_____

Explore your emotions! Write about the feelings that you experience each day, and why you felt them.

M T W T F S S   ___/___/___

M T W T F S S   ___/___/___

M T W T F S S   ___/___/___

M T W T F S S   ___/___/___

M T W T F S S   ___/___/___

M T W T F S S   ___/___/___

M T W T F S S   ___/___/___

Write about a close friend and three qualities you admire in them.

_____

_____

_____

_____

_____

_____

_____

_____

_____

_____

Feelings Challenge!

Tell your friend the three qualities you admire in them.

Smile Tracker!

This week, I smiled when _____

_____

_____

Explore your emotions! Write about the feelings that you experience each day, and why you felt them.

M T W T F S S	___/___/___

M T W T F S S	___/___/___

M T W T F S S	___/___/___

Think of a feeling you had this month. Imagine if that feeling were a character. Draw a picture of that feelings character and include a bubble showing what they might think or say.

Mood Log for the Month of
_____!

Each box below represents a day this month. Every day draw how you feel.

HAPPY	SAD	SILLY	ANGRY	DISAPPOINTED	FRUSTRATED
GRATEFUL	ANXIOUS	SURPRISED	EXCITED	SCARED	PROUD

1	2	3	4	5	6	7
8	9	10	11	12	13	14
15	16	17	18	19	20	21
22	23	24	25	26	27	28
29	30	31				

What was the feeling you had the most this month? _____

_____

Explore your emotions! Write about the feelings that you experience each day, and why you felt them.

M T W T F S S   ___/___/___

M T W T F S S   ___/___/___

M T W T F S S   ___/___/___

M T W T F S S   ___/___/___

M T W T F S S   ___/___/___

M T W T F S S   ___/___/___

M T W T F S S   ___/___/___

When have you felt nervous about something? Did the thing turn out to be as bad as you thought?

_____

_____

_____

_____

_____

_____

_____

_____

_____

Feelings Challenge!

Think about something that makes you nervous. Practice in front of a mirror telling yourself things that help.

Smile Tracker!

This week, I smiled when _____

_____

_____

Explore your emotions! Write about the feelings that you experience each day, and why you felt them.

M T W T F S S   __/__/__

M T W T F S S   __/__/__

M T W T F S S   __/__/__

M T W T F S S   __/__/__

M T W T F S S   __/__/__

M T W T F S S   __/__/__

M T W T F S S   __/__/__

Write about three things in your life that you are grateful for.

_____

_____

_____

_____

_____

_____

_____

_____

_____

_____

Feelings Challenge!

Tell your parents or guardian three specific things you appreciate about them. How does it feel to share?

Smile Tracker!

This week, I smiled when _____

_____

_____

Explore your emotions! Write about the feelings that you experience each day, and why you felt them.

M T W T F S S   ___/___/___

M T W T F S S   ___/___/___

M T W T F S S   ___/___/___

M T W T F S S   ___/___/___

M T W T F S S   ___/___/___

M T W T F S S   ___/___/___

M T W T F S S   ___/___/___

When was a time that you felt disgusted? What did that feel like?

_____

_____

_____

_____

_____

_____

_____

_____

_____

Feelings Challenge!

Look at something you find disgusting. Notice what happens in your body.

Smile Tracker!

This week, I smiled when _____

_____

_____

Explore your emotions! Write about the feelings that you experience each day, and why you felt them.

M T W T F S S   ___/___/___

M T W T F S S   ___/___/___

M T W T F S S   ___/___/___

M T W T F S S   ___/___/___

M T W T F S S   ___/___/___

M T W T F S S   ___/___/___

M T W T F S S   ___/___/___

Write about a time when you have felt love for someone. What does love feel like inside?

_____

_____

_____

_____

_____

_____

_____

_____

_____

Feelings Challenge!

Make up a song about love, and share it with a friend or sibling.

Smile Tracker!

This week, I smiled when _____

_____

_____

Explore your emotions! Write about the feelings that you experience each day, and why you felt them.

M T W T F S S	___/___/___

M T W T F S S	___/___/___

M T W T F S S	___/___/___

Think of a feeling you had this month. Imagine if that feeling were a character. Draw a picture of that feelings character and include a bubble showing what they might think or say.

Mood Log for the Month of

_____!

Each box below represents a day this month. Every day draw how you feel.

| HAPPY | SAD | SILLY | ANGRY | DISAPPOINTED | FRUSTRATED |
| GRATEFUL | ANXIOUS | SURPRISED | EXCITED | SCARED | PROUD |

1	2	3	4	5	6	7
8	9	10	11	12	13	14
15	16	17	18	19	20	21
22	23	24	25	26	27	28
29	30	31				

What was the feeling you had the most this month? _____

_____

Explore your emotions! Write about the feelings that you experience each day, and why you felt them.

MTWTFSS ___/___/___

MTWTFSS ___/___/___

MTWTFSS ___/___/___

MTWTFSS ___/___/___

MTWTFSS ___/___/___

MTWTFSS ___/___/___

MTWTFSS ___/___/___

Write about the feelings you felt at a time when you had to try something new.

_____

_____

_____

_____

_____

_____

_____

_____

Feelings Challenge!

1. Imagine trying something new that would be good for you to try.

2. Pick three things you could say to yourself to encourage yourself to try it.

3. Now sing those things to yourself as a made-up song.

Smile Tracker!

This week, I smiled when _____

_____

_____

Explore your emotions! Write about the feelings that you experience each day, and why you felt them.

MTWTFSS   ___/___/___

MTWTFSS   ___/___/___

MTWTFSS   ___/___/___

MTWTFSS   ___/___/___

MTWTFSS   ___/___/___

MTWTFSS   ___/___/___

MTWTFSS   ___/___/___

What advice would you give to someone who feels lonely?

_____

_____

_____

_____

_____

_____

_____

_____

_____

Feelings Challenge!

On small slips of paper, write down ideas for things that help when you're feeling lonely. Put the papers in a jar or box and decorate it. Take out and read a slip of paper any time you feel lonely.

Smile Tracker!

This week, I smiled when _____

_____

_____

Explore your emotions! Write about the feelings that you experience each day, and why you felt them.

MTWTFSS   ___/___/___

MTWTFSS   ___/___/___

MTWTFSS   ___/___/___

MTWTFSS   ___/___/___

MTWTFSS   ___/___/___

MTWTFSS   ___/___/___

MTWTFSS   ___/___/___

Write about something you did that you feel guilty about.

_____

_____

_____

_____

_____

_____

_____

_____

_____

_____

Feelings Challenge!

Apologize to yourself or another person who was affected by the thing you did. Be specific about the impact of what you did and what you will do differently in the future.

Smile Tracker!

This week, I smiled when _____

_____

_____

Explore your emotions! Write about the feelings that you experience each day, and why you felt them.

M T W T F S S ___ / ___ / ___

M T W T F S S ___ / ___ / ___

M T W T F S S ___ / ___ / ___

M T W T F S S ___ / ___ / ___

M T W T F S S ___ / ___ / ___

M T W T F S S ___ / ___ / ___

M T W T F S S ___ / ___ / ___

Write about when you feel most calm. What are you doing in that moment? Where are you?

_____

_____

_____

_____

_____

_____

_____

_____

_____

Feelings Challenge!

Lie down on the floor, close your eyes, and listen to a song that helps you feel calm.

Smile Tracker!

This week, I smiled when _____

_____

_____

Explore your emotions! Write about the feelings that you experience each day, and why you felt them.

M T W T F S S ___/___/___

M T W T F S S ___/___/___

M T W T F S S ___/___/___

Think of a feeling you had this month. Imagine if that feeling were a character. Draw a picture of that feelings character and include a bubble showing what they might think or say.

Mood Log for the Month of

_____!

Each box below represents a day this month. Every day draw how you feel.

🙂 HAPPY	😔 SAD	😜 SILLY	😠 ANGRY	🙁 DISAPPOINTED	😒 FRUSTRATED
😊 GRATEFUL	😬 ANXIOUS	😮 SURPRISED	😁 EXCITED	😧 SCARED	😎 PROUD

1	2	3	4	5	6	7
8	9	10	11	12	13	14
15	16	17	18	19	20	21
22	23	24	25	26	27	28
29	30	31				

What was the feeling you had the most this month? _____

_____

Explore your emotions! Write about the feelings that you experience each day, and why you felt them.

M T W T F S S   ___ / ___ / ___

M T W T F S S   ___ / ___ / ___

M T W T F S S   ___ / ___ / ___

M T W T F S S   ___ / ___ / ___

M T W T F S S   ___ / ___ / ___

M T W T F S S   ___ / ___ / ___

M T W T F S S   ___ / ___ / ___

Have you experienced anxiety before talking in front of a group? What helped you feel better?

_____

_____

_____

_____

_____

_____

_____

_____

_____

Feelings Challenge!

Imagine a white light is slowly traveling down your body. Tell each body part to relax as the light touches it.

Smile Tracker!

This week, I smiled when _____

_____

_____

Explore your emotions! Write about the feelings that you experience each day, and why you felt them.

MTWTFSS ___/___/___

MTWTFSS ___/___/___

MTWTFSS ___/___/___

MTWTFSS ___/___/___

MTWTFSS ___/___/___

MTWTFSS ___/___/___

MTWTFSS ___/___/___

Write about a time when feeling curious got you in trouble.

_____

_____

_____

_____

_____

_____

_____

_____

_____

Feelings Challenge!

Check out a book from the library on something you are curious about.

Smile Tracker!

This week, I smiled when _____

_____

_____

Explore your emotions! Write about the feelings that you experience each day, and why you felt them.

M T W T F S S   ___ / ___ / ___

M T W T F S S   ___ / ___ / ___

M T W T F S S   ___ / ___ / ___

M T W T F S S   ___ / ___ / ___

M T W T F S S   ___ / ___ / ___

M T W T F S S   ___ / ___ / ___

M T W T F S S   ___ / ___ / ___

Write about a time in school when you felt confused. What thoughts did that make you have about yourself?

_____

_____

_____

_____

_____

_____

_____

_____

_____

Feelings Challenge!

The next time you feel confused in the classroom, raise your hand and ask for clarification.

Smile Tracker!

This week, I smiled when _____

_____

_____

Explore your emotions! Write about the feelings that you experience each day, and why you felt them.

M T W T F S S   ___ / ___ / ___

M T W T F S S   ___ / ___ / ___

M T W T F S S   ___ / ___ / ___

M T W T F S S   ___ / ___ / ___

M T W T F S S   ___ / ___ / ___

M T W T F S S   ___ / ___ / ___

M T W T F S S   ___ / ___ / ___

When have you had a conflict with a friend? What feelings came up?

_____

_____

_____

_____

_____

_____

_____

_____

Feelings Challenge!

Try apologizing to somebody by doing a nice thing for them. When you do it, apologize for what you did and let the person know you are doing this nice thing because you care about them.

Smile Tracker!

This week, I smiled when _____

_____

_____

Explore your emotions! Write about the feelings that you experience each day, and why you felt them.

M T W T F S S	___ / ___ / ___

M T W T F S S	___ / ___ / ___

M T W T F S S	___ / ___ / ___

Think of a feeling you had this month. Imagine if that feeling were a character. Draw a picture of that feelings character and include a bubble showing what they might think or say.

Mood Log for the Month of
_____ !

Each box below represents a day this month. Every day draw how you feel.

HAPPY	SAD	SILLY	ANGRY	DISAPPOINTED	FRUSTRATED
GRATEFUL	ANXIOUS	SURPRISED	EXCITED	SCARED	PROUD

1	2	3	4	5	6	7
8	9	10	11	12	13	14
15	16	17	18	19	20	21
22	23	24	25	26	27	28
29	30	31				

What was the feeling you had the most this month? _____

_____

Explore your emotions! Write about the feelings that you experience each day, and why you felt them.

M T W T F S S ___/___/___

M T W T F S S ___/___/___

M T W T F S S ___/___/___

M T W T F S S ___/___/___

M T W T F S S ___/___/___

M T W T F S S ___/___/___

M T W T F S S ___/___/___

"Pessimism" is the feeling you have when you really focus on the negatives in a situation and expect something bad will happen. Write about a time when you felt pessimistic. How did it change how you acted?

_____

_____

_____

_____

_____

Feelings Challenge!

Next time you feel pessimistic, ask yourself these questions:

1. What is the worst thing that could happen?

2. On a scale of 1 to 10, how likely is that to happen?

3. What would I do if that actually happened?

4. What are some other possibilities of things that could happen?

Smile Tracker!

This week, I smiled when _____

_____

_____

Explore your emotions! Write about the feelings that you experience each day, and why you felt them.

M T W T F S S ___/___/___

M T W T F S S ___/___/___

M T W T F S S ___/___/___

M T W T F S S ___/___/___

M T W T F S S ___/___/___

M T W T F S S ___/___/___

M T W T F S S ___/___/___

"Optimism" is a feeling of hopefulness and confidence about the future. Write about something that you are feeling optimistic about. What makes you optimistic?

_____

_____

_____

_____

_____

_____

Feelings Challenge!

Next time you notice someone in your life being pessimistic, try this:

1. Tell them you're sorry they're feeling down.

2. Ask them why they're feeling that way.

3. Tell them some reasons they can "look on the bright side" (looking on the bright side means being optimistic).

Smile Tracker!

This week, I smiled when _____

_____

_____

Explore your emotions! Write about the feelings that you experience each day, and why you felt them.

M T W T F S S   ___ / ___ / ___

M T W T F S S   ___ / ___ / ___

M T W T F S S   ___ / ___ / ___

M T W T F S S   ___ / ___ / ___

M T W T F S S   ___ / ___ / ___

M T W T F S S   ___ / ___ / ___

M T W T F S S   ___ / ___ / ___

Think of a time when you felt anxious. What was causing it? What helped you feel better?

_____

_____

_____

_____

_____

_____

_____

_____

Feelings Challenge!

Practice box breathing: Breathe in, counting to four slowly, then hold your breath for four counts, and finally breathe out for four counts. Repeat five times.

Smile Tracker!

This week, I smiled when _____

_____

_____

Explore your emotions! Write about the feelings that you experience each day, and why you felt them.

M T W T F S S ___/___/___

M T W T F S S ___/___/___

M T W T F S S ___/___/___

M T W T F S S ___/___/___

M T W T F S S ___/___/___

M T W T F S S ___/___/___

M T W T F S S ___/___/___

If your worry were a character, who would it be and why?

_____

_____

_____

_____

_____

_____

_____

Feelings Challenge!

Next time you feel worried about something, try this:

1. Close your eyes and take three deep breaths.

2. Each time you have a worrying thought, imagine the thought is written on a balloon, and watch it float up into the sky. You don't need to get rid of it or change it. Just watch it float away.

Smile Tracker!

This week, I smiled when _____

_____

_____

Explore your emotions! Write about the feelings that you experience each day, and why you felt them.

| M T W T F S S | ___/___/___ |
| | |

| M T W T F S S | ___/___/___ |
| | |

| M T W T F S S | ___/___/___ |
| | |

Think of a feeling you had this month. Imagine if that feeling were a character. Draw a picture of that feelings character and include a bubble showing what they might think or say.

Mood Log for the Month of

_____!

Each box below represents a day this month. Every day draw how you feel.

HAPPY	SAD	SILLY	ANGRY	DISAPPOINTED	FRUSTRATED
GRATEFUL	ANXIOUS	SURPRISED	EXCITED	SCARED	PROUD

1	2	3	4	5	6	7
8	9	10	11	12	13	14
15	16	17	18	19	20	21
22	23	24	25	26	27	28
29	30	31				

What was the feeling you had the most this month? _____

_____

Explore your emotions! Write about the feelings that you experience each day, and why you felt them.

MTWTFSS   ___/___/___

MTWTFSS   ___/___/___

MTWTFSS   ___/___/___

MTWTFSS   ___/___/___

MTWTFSS   ___/___/___

MTWTFSS   ___/___/___

MTWTFSS   ___/___/___

Write about a person, animal, or beloved item you lost. Why were they important to you?

_____

_____

_____

_____

_____

_____

_____

_____

_____

Feelings Challenge!

Honor this person, animal, or thing with a letter, blessing, drawing, or ceremony.

Smile Tracker!

This week, I smiled when _____

_____

_____

Explore your emotions! Write about the feelings that you experience each day, and why you felt them.

MTWTFSS   ___/___/___

MTWTFSS   ___/___/___

MTWTFSS   ___/___/___

MTWTFSS   ___/___/___

MTWTFSS   ___/___/___

MTWTFSS   ___/___/___

MTWTFSS   ___/___/___

What are three feelings that come up when you think of a sibling, a cousin, or another family member? Why?

_____

_____

_____

_____

_____

_____

_____

_____

_____

Feelings Challenge!

Tell your sibling, cousin, or other family member three specific things that you appreciate about them.

Smile Tracker!

This week, I smiled when _____

_____

_____

Explore your emotions! Write about the feelings that you experience each day, and why you felt them.

M T W T F S S   ___/___/___

M T W T F S S   ___/___/___

M T W T F S S   ___/___/___

M T W T F S S   ___/___/___

M T W T F S S   ___/___/___

M T W T F S S   ___/___/___

M T W T F S S   ___/___/___

Write about the feelings you had joining a new group for the first time. This could have been a new class, sports team, club, camp, or any other new activity.

_____

_____

_____

_____

_____

_____

_____

_____

Feelings Challenge!

Ask a friend how they felt when they joined a new group. Share your experience in return!

Smile Tracker!

This week, I smiled when _____

_____

_____

Explore your emotions! Write about the feelings that you experience each day, and why you felt them.

M T W T F S S   ___ / ___ / ___

M T W T F S S   ___ / ___ / ___

M T W T F S S   ___ / ___ / ___

M T W T F S S   ___ / ___ / ___

M T W T F S S   ___ / ___ / ___

M T W T F S S   ___ / ___ / ___

M T W T F S S   ___ / ___ / ___

Write about a time when you had two or more very different feelings at once.

_____

_____

_____

_____

_____

_____

_____

_____

Feelings Challenge!

Next time you have a strong feeling, ask yourself if you have any other feelings at the same time. Identify where you feel each of the different feelings in your body.

Smile Tracker!

This week, I smiled when _____

_____

_____

Explore your emotions! Write about the feelings that you experience each day, and why you felt them.

MTWTFSS   ___/___/___

MTWTFSS   ___/___/___

MTWTFSS   ___/___/___

Think of a feeling you had this month. Imagine if that feeling were a character. Draw a picture of that feelings character and include a bubble showing what they might think or say.

Mood Log for the Month of

_____ !

Each box below represents a day this month. Every day draw how you feel.

HAPPY	SAD	SILLY	ANGRY	DISAPPOINTED	FRUSTRATED
GRATEFUL	ANXIOUS	SURPRISED	EXCITED	SCARED	PROUD

1	2	3	4	5	6	7
8	9	10	11	12	13	14
15	16	17	18	19	20	21
22	23	24	25	26	27	28
29	30	31				

What was the feeling you had the most this month? _____

_____

Explore your emotions! Write about the feelings that you experience each day, and why you felt them.

M T W T F S S   ___/___/___

M T W T F S S   ___/___/___

M T W T F S S   ___/___/___

M T W T F S S   ___/___/___

M T W T F S S   ___/___/___

M T W T F S S   ___/___/___

M T W T F S S   ___/___/___

Write about something you're afraid of and why.

_____

_____

_____

_____

_____

_____

_____

_____

_____

_____

Feelings Challenge!

Make up a silly song about the thing you're afraid of. Does singing your song make that thing less scary?

Smile Tracker!

This week, I smiled when _____

_____

_____

Explore your emotions! Write about the feelings that you experience each day, and why you felt them.

MTWTFSS   ___/___/___

MTWTFSS   ___/___/___

MTWTFSS   ___/___/___

MTWTFSS   ___/___/___

MTWTFSS   ___/___/___

MTWTFSS   ___/___/___

MTWTFSS   ___/___/___

When have you thought you'd have one feeling about something but ended up experiencing a different feeling?

_____

_____

_____

_____

_____

_____

_____

_____

Feelings Challenge!

Practice three dragon breaths. For each, inhale slowly and exhale with your mouth open and your tongue out.

Smile Tracker!

This week, I smiled when _____

_____

_____

Explore your emotions! Write about the feelings that you experience each day, and why you felt them.

M T W T F S S   ___ / ___ / ___

M T W T F S S   ___ / ___ / ___

M T W T F S S   ___ / ___ / ___

M T W T F S S   ___ / ___ / ___

M T W T F S S   ___ / ___ / ___

M T W T F S S   ___ / ___ / ___

M T W T F S S   ___ / ___ / ___

Write about a dream you had and identify three feelings it caused.

_____

_____

_____

_____

_____

_____

_____

_____

_____

_____

Feelings Challenge!

Draw a picture of a scene from your dream.

Smile Tracker!

This week, I smiled when _____

_____

_____

Explore your emotions! Write about the feelings that you experience each day, and why you felt them.

M T W T F S S   ___/___/___

M T W T F S S   ___/___/___

M T W T F S S   ___/___/___

M T W T F S S   ___/___/___

M T W T F S S   ___/___/___

M T W T F S S   ___/___/___

M T W T F S S   ___/___/___

Write about a time when a mood you were in influenced how you acted.

_____

_____

_____

_____

_____

_____

_____

_____

_____

Feelings Challenge!

Listen to three songs you like, and identify what the moods of the songs are.

Smile Tracker!

This week, I smiled when _____

_____

_____

Explore your emotions! Write about the feelings that you experience each day, and why you felt them.

M T W T F S S   ___/___/___

M T W T F S S   ___/___/___

M T W T F S S   ___/___/___

Think of a feeling you had this month. Imagine if that feeling were a character. Draw a picture of that feelings character and include a bubble showing what they might think or say.

Mood Log for the Month of

_____ !

Each box below represents a day this month. Every day draw how you feel.

HAPPY	SAD	SILLY	ANGRY	DISAPPOINTED	FRUSTRATED
GRATEFUL	ANXIOUS	SURPRISED	EXCITED	SCARED	PROUD

1	2	3	4	5	6	7
8	9	10	11	12	13	14
15	16	17	18	19	20	21
22	23	24	25	26	27	28
29	30	31				

What was the feeling you had the most this month? _____

_____

Explore your emotions! Write about the feelings that you experience each day, and why you felt them.

M T W T F S S   ___/___/___

M T W T F S S   ___/___/___

M T W T F S S   ___/___/___

M T W T F S S   ___/___/___

M T W T F S S   ___/___/___

M T W T F S S   ___/___/___

M T W T F S S   ___/___/___

Write about a time you were having a bad day but then it turned around. What made you start to feel better?

_____

_____

_____

_____

_____

_____

_____

_____

_____

Feelings Challenge!

The next time you're having a bad day, try to remember what you can do to make yourself feel better. Then do it!

Smile Tracker!

This week, I smiled when _____

_____

_____

Explore your emotions! Write about the feelings that you experience each day, and why you felt them.

M T W T F S S   ___ / ___ / ___

M T W T F S S   ___ / ___ / ___

M T W T F S S   ___ / ___ / ___

M T W T F S S   ___ / ___ / ___

M T W T F S S   ___ / ___ / ___

M T W T F S S   ___ / ___ / ___

M T W T F S S   ___ / ___ / ___

Write about a person in your life who you're not close to but usually makes you feel good—like your school bus driver or a kid in another class. What do they do that makes you feel good?

_____

_____

_____

_____

_____

_____

_____

Feelings Challenge!

Pay it forward! Try doing some of the things that person does that make you feel good back to them or to other people in your life.

Smile Tracker!

This week, I smiled when _____

_____

_____

Explore your emotions! Write about the feelings that you experience each day, and why you felt them.

M T W T F S S   ___/___/___

M T W T F S S   ___/___/___

M T W T F S S   ___/___/___

M T W T F S S   ___/___/___

M T W T F S S   ___/___/___

M T W T F S S   ___/___/___

M T W T F S S   ___/___/___

Write about a time you had a really big feeling but didn't know why you were feeling that way.

_____

_____

_____

_____

_____

_____

_____

_____

Feelings Challenge!

The next time you feel overwhelmed by a big feeling, try stepping back. Go to a quiet place to work through what you're feeling. If you're with another person, you can say, "I need some time to process what I'm feeling right now."

Smile Tracker!

This week, I smiled when _____

_____

_____

Explore your emotions! Write about the feelings that you experience each day, and why you felt them.

M T W T F S S   ___/___/___

M T W T F S S   ___/___/___

M T W T F S S   ___/___/___

M T W T F S S   ___/___/___

M T W T F S S   ___/___/___

M T W T F S S   ___/___/___

M T W T F S S   ___/___/___

When do you feel most free to be yourself? Why do you think that is?

_____

_____

_____

_____

_____

_____

_____

_____

Feelings Challenge!

If it feels safe, try being yourself a bit more freely in situations that have challenged you in the past. Notice how you feel.

Smile Tracker!

This week, I smiled when _____

_____

_____

Explore your emotions! Write about the feelings that you experience each day, and why you felt them.

MTWTFSS ___/___/___

MTWTFSS ___/___/___

MTWTFSS ___/___/___

Think of a feeling you had this month. Imagine if that feeling were a character. Draw a picture of that feelings character and include a bubble showing what they might think or say.

Mood Log for the Month of
_____!

Each box below represents a day this month. Every day draw how you feel.

HAPPY	SAD	SILLY	ANGRY	DISAPPOINTED	FRUSTRATED
GRATEFUL	ANXIOUS	SURPRISED	EXCITED	SCARED	PROUD

1	2	3	4	5	6	7
8	9	10	11	12	13	14
15	16	17	18	19	20	21
22	23	24	25	26	27	28
29	30	31				

What was the feeling you had the most this month? _____

_____

What are some things that you learned about yourself and your feelings from writing in this journal?

_____

_____

_____

_____

_____

_____

_____

_____

_____

_____

_____

_____

_____

_____

_____

_____

_____

_____

What Feelings Challenges in this journal did you enjoy most and why?

_____

_____

_____

_____

_____

_____

_____

_____

_____

_____

_____

_____

_____

_____

_____

_____

_____

_____

_____

What three feelings are hardest for you to process? Why do you think that is?

_____

_____

_____

_____

_____

_____

_____

_____

_____

_____

_____

_____

_____

_____

_____

_____

_____

_____

Write a story of an epic battle between two feelings based on your experiences!

_____

_____

_____

_____

_____

_____

_____

_____

_____

_____

_____

_____

_____

_____

_____

_____

_____

_____

Are your feelings usually your friends or your enemies? Why?

_____

_____

_____

_____

_____

_____

_____

_____

_____

_____

_____

_____

_____

_____

_____

_____

_____

_____

_____

Some people say all feelings are important. Do you agree or disagree? Why?

_____

_____

_____

_____

_____

_____

_____

_____

_____

_____

_____

_____

_____

_____

_____

_____

_____

_____

How do you imagine life would be different if you didn't have feelings?

_____

_____

_____

_____

_____

_____

_____

_____

_____

_____

_____

_____

_____

_____

_____

_____

_____

_____

Write a poem about a feeling that became so big you had to
do something about it.

_____

_____

_____

_____

_____

_____

_____

_____

_____

_____

_____

_____

_____

_____

_____

_____

_____

_____

Do you believe other animals have the same feelings as humans? Why or why not? How can you tell?

_____

_____

_____

_____

_____

_____

_____

_____

_____

_____

_____

_____

_____

_____

_____

_____

_____

Now that you're a feelings expert, write a letter to an imaginary person who struggles with big feelings and give them advice.

_____

_____

_____

_____

_____

_____

_____

_____

_____

_____

_____

_____

_____

_____

_____

_____

_____

_____

About the Author

 **Nathan Greene, PsyD,** is a clinical psychologist in private practice in Oakland, California, where he provides psychotherapy to children, adolescents, and adults. He is a cofounder and facilitator of Surf Circle, a therapeutic surf program for adolescent boys, which combines surf lessons and group therapy on the beach. Alongside his clinical work, Dr. Greene teaches clinical psychology doctoral students at the Wright Institute in Berkeley and serves on the Medical Affairs Team for Healthline Media. Outside of the office, he can be found surfing and hiking around the Bay Area with his two loves, one fluffy and one human. Get in touch with Dr. Greene and learn about his work at DrNathanGreene.com and SurfCircle.org.

CPSIA information can be obtained
at www.ICGtesting.com
Printed in the USA
BVHW021123220122
626735BV00017B/275